FLEETWOOL MAC

GREATEST HITS

Photography: Herbert W. Worthington III

Photography: Sam Emerson

Photography: Neal Preston

Photography: Norman Seeff

Photography: Sam Emerson

Wembley, northern London, late May of Eighty Eight. England plays Scotland for UK football bragging rights on Saturday and huge colored banners wave smartly in the wind atop the parapets of the stadium. Tango In The Night is the number one record in England for the second time, and Fleetwood Mac has sold out ten nights at Wembley Arena, eight years after last playing in its native land. ♣ "Thirty minutes" calls Wayne Cody, continuing his traditional countdown to showtime. An hour earlier Fleetwood Mac (Mark XI) has convened onstage for the day's soundcheck and a brief rehearsal. For twenty minutes the great band burns away to the giant empty hall, stopping to re-weave the three voice harmony to their current British hit single: "Tell me lies, tell me sweet little lies . . ." ♣ Now the band and its corps of rock soldiers are pacing and chatting and waiting out the anxious minutes right before a show. And there's cause for some nervousness. A royal prince has tickets tonight and has been invited backstage after the show. And there are the fans, some of whom have been paying to see Fleetwood Mac for more than twenty years. The backstage consensus is that tonight would not be a good night for a less-than-magic show. ♣ Twenty minutes! ♣ John McVie sits in the dressing room, smoking, relaxed, tight but loose. He says that when he was asked to join Fleetwood Mac during the summer of 1967, he declined and took a kif holiday in Morocco instead. Mick Fleetwood, six feet six inches of King Lear intensity, studies his costume and makeup in the mirror, issues many vague orders and great oaths, and says something about the wild days of the young Mac in the sixties. Christine Perfect McVie slips into the men's dressing room with a knowing smile. Slender, beautiful and elegant, she banters with the boys, her regal but unassuming demeanor instantly grabbing the moment. ♣ Stevie Nicks is in the dressing room she shares with Christine; she is not to be seen, preferring to prepare for Fleetwood Mac's return in seclusion, like a bride. ♣ Ten Minutes . . . ♣ Back in the boy's room Billy Burnette is trying on a black silk shirt from a shop in Bond Street. Three hundred and fifty quid for a shirt, but Billy's band has sold out 10 nights at Wembley so it's OK. With a laugh and a flash of black eyes, Mr. Burnette, a real gentleman, accepts the B12 shot offered by the comical English tour doc. New guitarist Rick Vito sits next to Mick at the mirror. As a teenager in Philadelphia he paid to see the original Mac in 1968 when they were just becoming known in the States. Playing here in London Rick Vito has a strange feeling, as though he were stepping into some pretty heavy shoes indeed. ♣ Five minutes! ♣ Last second bustle. Over in the corner the brilliant Ghanaian drummer Isaac Asante adjusts his horned cowrie-shell helmet. Mick has finished his toilette and is high-stepping in place and howling. Band managers John Courage, Dennis Dunstan and Tony Dimitriades issue final instructions to the crew and hall personnel. The dressing rooms feel electric, supercharged. And one almost senses the ghosts in the band, those not present, but there all the same in spirit: the magisterial young blues god Peter Green; Jeremy Spencer, child of God; Danny Kirwan, whose playing was like blue water under Peter's red fire; Bob Welch, the California mystician; and Lindsey Buckingham, Fleetwood Mac's protean guitarist and singer for more than a decade. ♣ Two minutes, and Fleetwood Mac files breathlessly into the shadows behind the big raised stage. Ziggy Marley fades off the PA . . . house lights dim as crew climb rope ladders like spider monkeys . . . thousands of voices roar for the music as Rick plays a chord and Mick starts the rhythm and suddenly it's Fleetwood Mac in full throttle at top volume. "'Cause when the loving starts, and the lights go down, and there's not another living soul around . . . and you say that you love me." Chris is singing the lead, and Stevie chants amidst a wonderful stagelit luminescence about her noble, golden head. Ten rows back are her true fans, clad in top hats and chiffon scarves; they remember the days when Rhiannon the Welsh mare-goddess alighted onstage like a dark-winged apparition during Fleetwood Mac shows past. ♣ For two hours, Fleetwood Mac holds its audience in thrall. Billy sings Lindsey's parts in "The Chain," and it's real. Stevie sings "Dreams" and gets an ovation. "Isn't it midnight, on the other side of the world?" Mick and Stevie rock "Sara," drowning in the sea of love. Billy Burnette does Peter Green's "Oh Well" and gets a big cheer. Same for Stevie's "Seven Wonders." Rick Vito pays his tribute to the early Mac with "Stop Messing Around" and "I Loved Another Woman." In quick succession: "Over My Head" with its bell-clear harmonies, "Gold Dust Woman," "Don't Let Me Down," and the lovely "Has Anyone Ever Written" which ends with Stevie's recitative that holds the crowd silent, spellbound. This mood is sustained as Chris sings the glorious "Brown Eyes," her blue alto lightly dipped in melancholy. But Mick changes everything as he and Asante put on a solo drum show during "World Turning." Playing touch-sensitive drum pads concealed in a vest, Mick grimaces and cavorts sending out jagged shards of sampled sounds. "Oh God," the vest screams when Mick thumps his chest. "Help Me!" He taps his tummy and you hear a car crash. It's a weird and wondrous techno-dance, rendered even stranger by the masked Asante's hand-drum mojo. ♣ Now the set builds to climax. "Little Lies" is right and tight. "Stand Back" is awesome. "You Make Loving Fun" is astral travel back to the spirit of Seventy Six. "Go Your Own Way" ends the show with a powerful rock son et lumiere. The encores: "Blue Letter," "Don't Stop," and, at the end Christine by herself at the piano, singing "Songbird" under a pencil spot, holding Fleetwood Mac's delirious crowd as if she were alone in some smokey dive, after hours. ♣ As she finishes, the audience lets loose. Delirium. John McVie introduces the band. Stevie and Chris receive standing ovations and many bouquets. Mick singles out the newest Macs, Burnette and Vito, for special praise. As the house lights come on, the somber tones of "Albatross" on the PA elicits a final cheer, Fleetwood Mac's perennial English top ten hit. ♣ Back in the dressing rooms, there's hot food and cold lager beer. The young prince is escorted to a reception room with his minders, his leather-jacketed girlfriend and his posh friends, to be introduced to the band. Mick makes sure Asante, a loyal citizen of the British Commonwealth, shakes hands with the prince. Handsome, balding slightly in the back like his brothers and father, the prince is cordial and complimentary, and the whole company is flattered that he came. ♣ As always, Mick Fleetwood is the last musician to leave the hall. As his Daimler limousine cuts through the wet nighttime streets of springtime London, Mick asks the driver to detour, and he rides through the Notting Hill Gate area where he first came to live as a fifteen-year-old Home Counties lad in 1963, smitten with the Beatles and ready to rock. ♣ And rock he did. ♣ The next night, after another successful show, Warner Bros. Records gives a party in Mac's honor at the Kensington Roof Gardens. The entertainment is an ace London boogie band and the members of Fleetwood Mac dance with each other until dawn. On my way home, I remember what an old friend of the band, Judy Wong, had told me a few months earlier. "There's a depth to this group," Judy said, "a zen-like pure flame of truth and a sense of destiny. People were meant to be in the band. No one ever auditioned, musicians were hired on intuition and instinct. Most of all, nothing ordinary ever happened to Fleetwood Mac." ♣ Those words still hold true, probably will for many years to come. It's too late to stop now.

STEPHEN DAVIS 1988

CONTENTS

RHIANNON

Words and Music by
STEVIE NICKS

Moderately, with a beat

Rhi - an - non rings like a bell through the night. And
She is like a cat in the dark, and

would-n't you love to love her?
then she is the dark - ness.

Takes to the sky like a
She rules her life like a

Will you ev - er win?__

Rhi - an - non.

Rhi - an - non.

Tak - en by, tak - en by the sky.__

DON'T STOP

Words and Music by
CHRISTINE McVIE

GO YOUR OWN WAY

Words and Music by
LINDSEY BUCKINGHAM

Moderately bright Rock beat

Lov - ing you is - n't the right___ thing_ to do.
Tell_ me why ev -'ry-thing turned_ a - round.

How can I _____ ev - er change things_ that_ I feel?_____
Pack - ing up,_____ shack - ing up is all you wan - na do._____

If_ I could,_____ may-be I'd give_____ you_ my world._____
If_ I could,_____ ba - by, I'd give_____ you_ my world._____

HOLD ME

Words and Music by
CHRISTINE McVIE and ROBBIE PATTON

EVERYWHERE

Words and Music by
CHRISTINE McVIE

'ry - where,__ I wan-na be with you ev - 'ry - where.

'ry - where.__ I wan-na be with you ev-

'ry-where.

D.S. %al Coda

Repeat and fade (Vocal ad lib)

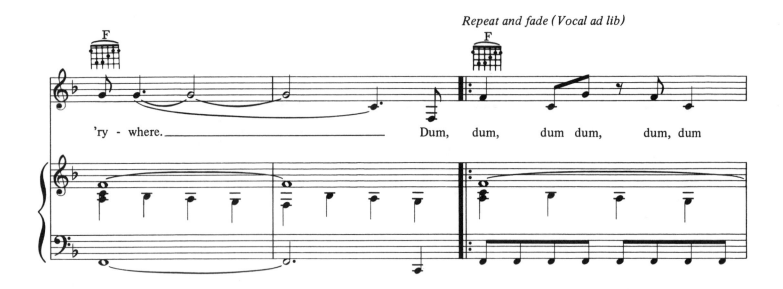

'ry - where._____ Dum, dum, dum dum, dum, dum

dum, dum, dum, dum, dum dum. Dum, dum, dum, dum, dum, dum, dum dum,

3rd Verse

Can you hear me calling
out you name?
You know that I'm falling
and I don't know what to say.

Come along baby
We better make a start.
You better make it soon
before you break my heart.

GYPSY

Words and Music by
STEVIE NICKS

to the vel - vet

un - der - ground,

back to the floor

that I love;

to a room

with some lace

and pa - per flow - ers;

back to the gyp -

Repeat (vocal ad lib) and fade

Vocal Ad Lib

Lightning strikes, maybe once, maybe twice.
And it all comes down to you.
I still see your bright eyes.
And it all comes down to you.

AS LONG AS YOU FOLLOW

Words and Music by
CHRISTINE McVIE and EDDY QUINTELA

Chorus:

Now I know I can't lose ___

___ as long ___ as you fol - low. ___

I'm ___ gon- na win, I'm gon- na beg, ___ steal or bor -

row ___ as long as you fol - low. ___

Now I know I can't lose,_

long as you fol - low;_

Repeat and fade

as long as you fol - low;_

SAY YOU LOVE ME

Words and Music by
CHRISTINE McVIE

DREAMS

Words and Music by
STEVIE NICKS

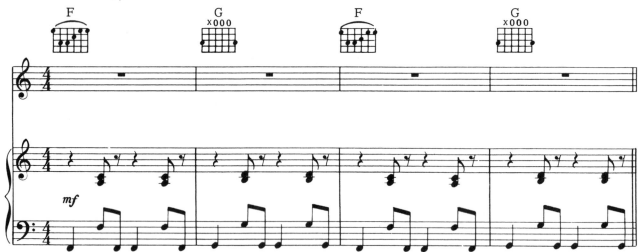

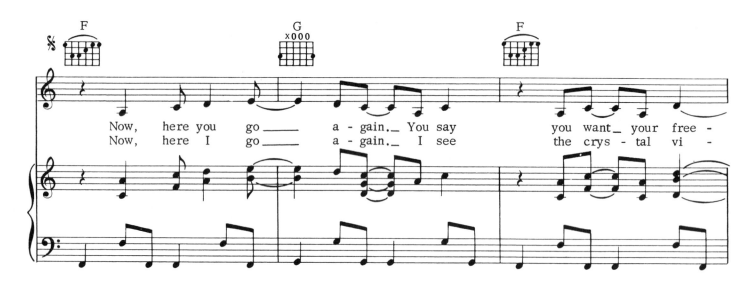

LITTLE LIES

Words by
CHRISTINE McVIE
Music by
CHRISTINE McVIE and EDDIE QUINTELA

SARA

Words and Music by
STEVIE NICKS

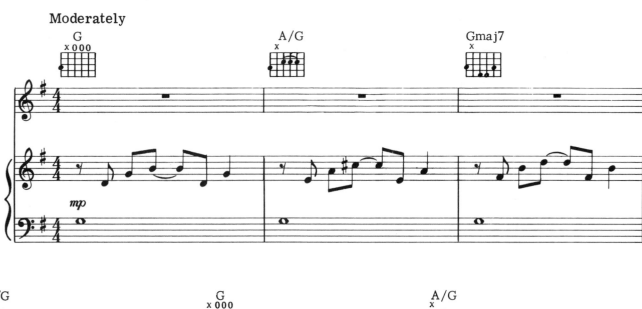

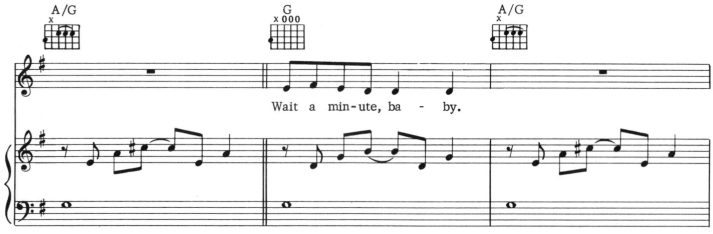

Wait a min-ute, ba - by.

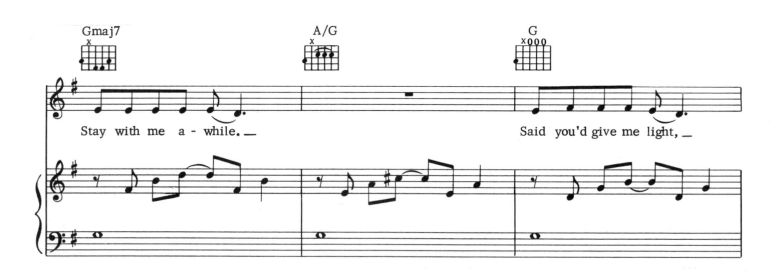

Stay with me a - while. ___   Said you'd give me light, ___

but you nev-er told ____ me 'bout the fire. ____

TUSK

Words and Music by
LINDSEY BUCKINGHAM

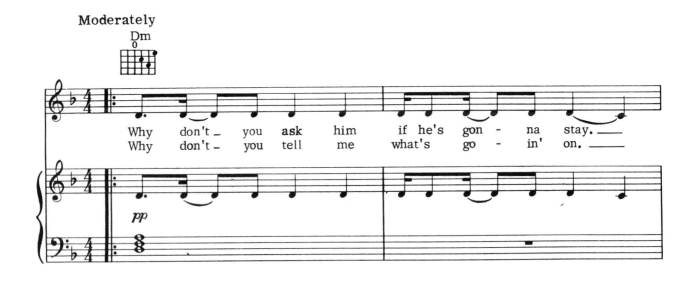

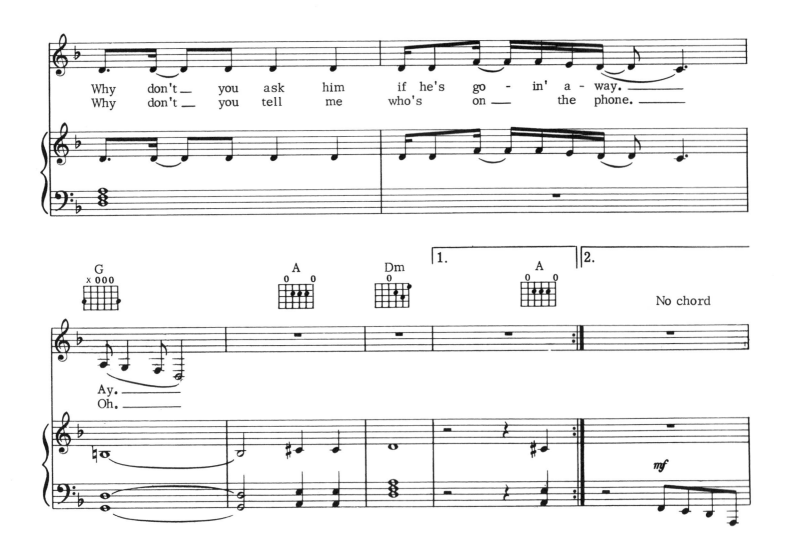

Why don't __ you ask him what's go - in' on. __

Why don't __ you ask him the lat -est on his throne. __ Oh, __

NO QUESTIONS ASKED

Words and Music by
STEVIE NICKS and KELLY JOHNSTON

Moderately fast rock

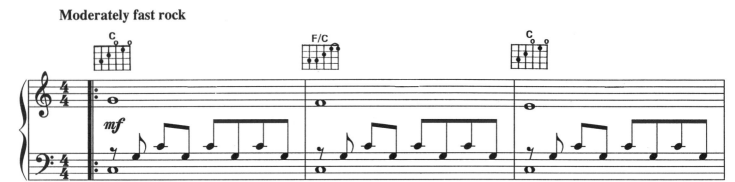

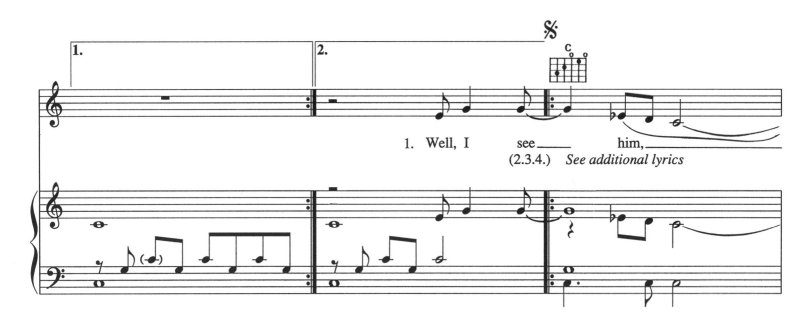

1. Well, I see____ him,____
(2.3.4.) *See additional lyrics*

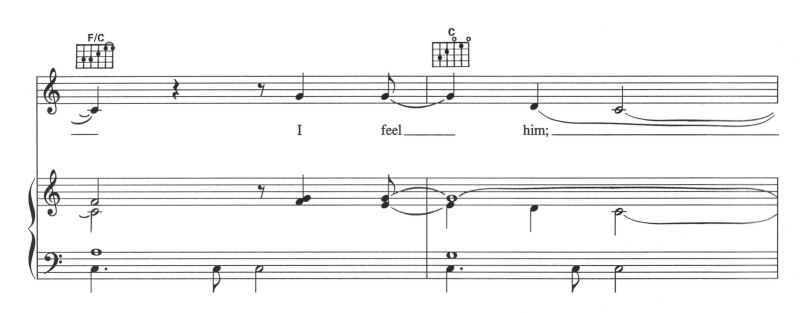

I feel____ him;____

no ques - tions asked; _____ well, I broke down _____

_____ like a lit - tle girl. _____

2. So how can you say,
   "Well, I don't know what love is"?
   You have it, and you have no time for it.
   You feel completely indifferent.
   You feel pushed up against the wall.
   And then one day it just almost goes away.

3. So, how can you say,
   "Well, I can't see you, not now,
   Not tomorrow, not until it's right,
   Not until neither of us is
   Pushed up against the wall"?
   I don't throw the cold winds of it
   At you . . . anymore.

4. So today she says,
   "Well, I changed my mind,
   That's a woman's right, they say."
   Well, I'm frightened and I'm lost
   And I can't give you up, not now.
   I need you now, I'm brokenhearted.
   I broke down like a little girl.